Det Var Livet Jeg Drømte Om

Anarky Taylor

BookLeaf Publishing

India | USA | UK

This book is dedicated to my parents,
I wouldn't be alive without you.

And to my grandparents,
for always reading whatever nonsense I
put in front of them, and for never giving
me a bad review.

THE JESTER

Begin,
Are you holding back?
Freedom,
Those reckless bones that crack.

There is spontaneity,
A wondrous fear of unknown,
Is it all worth the risk?
Ache to sit upon a throne?

Innocence,
Is naivety free?
Spirit,
The ignorance is key.

It is worth it at dusk,
That fleeting exhilarance.
Curiosity's tusk,
Mistaking its existence.

Piercing,
Wounds of now knowing,
Pain,

Price of disregarding.
Fools are selfish, aren't they?
Those that wonder and wander.
Their absence of concern,
Loved one's worrying ponder.

Angels,
Witness a tragedy.
Recklessness,
Ends in catastrophe.

There is a time and place,
For all your inquisition.
Where it provides insight,
Instead of a collision.

End,
Withhold to defend.
Contain,
For cautious bones do mend.

There lies a lesson,
And potential swims in blood.
You are the explorer,
Beware the potential flood.

THE CHARMER

Once Upon a time,
there was a charming evil.
Who lived in a fairy tale,
that was plenty deceitful.

Seldom a damsel,
comes to visit saving thoughts.
Playboy's decision,
"dashing" character to ties knots.

Interchangeable,
ladies foiled plans to meet.
Idealised subject,
"Prince" who took defeat.

This angers him so,
a man like him believing.
Beauty sees surface,
his irritating grieving.

There are variants,
this one happily charming.
Think him endearing,

love this fast is alarming.
Saving from worry,
He lacks an unwanted cause.
Handsome and loving,
so magnetic you don't pause.

Irreplaceable,
he could never disagree.
With this gentleman,
is an actuality.
This delights you so,
a man like him believing,
Beauty lies beneath,
with red cheeks, hearts are beating.

THE SACRED

There is something pleasantly rare
about intuition,
seems a withdrawal, a silent knowledge
of deeper understanding.
She calls it something of a premonition,
and secretly hoping to keep herself
standing.
Cares deeply but not of herself.

She cradles reflection dear to her
beating heart,
that uncertain hope for the opportunity
of retreat.
That fear which threatens to tear her
confidence apart,
To forge that self-certitude is no easy
feat.

That Lunar Crescent,
rests at her feet,
a false sense of passivity leaves
stillness,
upon her head.

Information withheld entices a sweet
mystery,
about how she acquired such a talent
for spiritual insight.
She houses an instinctual harmony,
She personifies that breeze of fresh air
of daylight.
But with the wisdom of the moon.

THE DIVINE

Ladies? Adversaries? Rivals?
Are words that should not be
synonymous.
None of those should go together.
Used to belittle and make anonymous.

As women, we are told not to be
successful.
"Don't strive to threaten the fragility,
It will make you undesirable and strong,
Shattering what is left of their
masculinity."

We are told that our only rival,
Is that of our fellow powerful women,
We must be envious of their bodies,
And how they attract and seduce men.

This shouldn't be our only mission,
There are so many things wrong with
the world,
There are bigger problems that we face,

So, our new agenda should now be
unfurled.

Women should have equal seats,
They should have a piece of their own
meal,
After all, didn't they serve what you are
about to eat?
Not be excluded only because they can
feel.

Women can have emotions and
strength,
It's not a rare chemical imbalance, you
know.
Embracing those thoughts and feelings
So that every night our hearts are aglow

We should be free to have our own
ambitions.
Not hide behind the looming shadows of
the other sex
We are just as creative, intelligent, and
powerful.
And should be shown and given equal
respect.

THE SACRIFICE

Who safeguards Hell?
Well, phone the girl with morning wings,
For she was raised in air,
To return.
She falls with malice like stones.
The whitening demon brought Valentine,
Pulling you curtly.
Reaching your hands.
Blood runs,
it's scalding.
Let him leave.
Make his veins embossed,
Demon valentine back home together.
Scarred
Ragged.
But it hurt.
Why?
Opportunity had hardly hinted,
She was lifted,
Chest lightless,
Crawling up.
Even in death searing,
His handsome eyes

Also sparkle better.
Than swaths of glass.
Once a graceful new pair,
You know one voice,
Over the blackish stare
With his raggedy jacket,
He restores the cross,
Quietly leaning close.

THE SOULS

Smell the gunpowder brass and blood,
he overloads your senses like a flood.
Clothes the scent of sandalwood and
books,
scarred skin that was pulled by hooks.
His face.

Touching him is grazing cold steel,
but hair and skin so smooth it's soft to
feel.
When you close your eyes, he is light in
dark,
with a hint of blue passing in a spark.
Can you see?

The Husky sound of his accent,
leaves you with the feeling of such
content.
Rarely it becomes a laugh,
would wait a lifetime and a half.
For him

Quips bitter than chocolate,

worse than carrying sea salt in your
pocket.
Eyes like his paler than icy water,
but love like caramel and rainwater.
Is he here?

THE AMBITIOUS

I wanna take my ego for a drive,
That seems a way to humble it,
So, it feels different when I arrive,
So, I'm not observing from the cockpit.

There are so many things I wish to be,
And so little time to genuinely think,
I can't figure out what it means to be
me,
Washing my ability down the kitchen
sink.

Is it procrastination that holds me back?
Or is it that crippling fear of failure,
Being afraid to even softly attack,
Biting the disappointed fisherman's lure.

It's been a while since I've reflected,
On the things that make me happy,
I'm becoming disconnected.
Frustration mirroring snappy.

I'll get there eventually,

I'm only young, yet,
Fearing existentially,
I bet.
That it is never easier.

I bet.

FORTUITOUS

Revolving wheel,
Each corner houses a creature,
A seat on a cloud they steal,
They are the mishaps of nature.

To be fortuitous,
One needs to understand luck,
The disappointment is carnivorous,
Misfortune runs amuck.

There is a secret,
Buried deep beneath the world,
Nothing needs chance's treatment,
The fear of destiny curled.

There is the unforeseen,
But does it really take precedence?
The whir of the broken machine,
You are luck's only influence.

MORTALITY

Have you ever thought about it?
Is there a "fate worse than death?"
I never bothered to admit that,
I fear taking that last breath.

Is it a little bit colder?
Than the winter back at home?
Is it comforting I wonder,
No longer able to roam.

PEACE

We were sitting alone on this park
bench,
We hadn't a clue of one another,
Merely sitting in comfortable silence,
Whistling of trees under the night sky.

I began to shift and shape paper in my
hands,
Until it began to resemble something of
a hat,
I made a noise of triumph, happy with
my work,
Headlights of the incoming train
illuminating it.

You gave me a brief glance when I
nudged your side,
Face slack, countenance stoic and
mouth set,
But eyes alive with wild curiosity,
You reached out gently and took it from
me.

You turned it around in your own hands
admiring it,
Head tilting in wonder from side to side,
You raised it above you with a tugging
smile,
And placed it upon your head without
another word.

It was something new to wear home.

THE TEMPTER

He represents many,
a man of temptation,
broken relationships,

feeling enslaved and trapped?
but is also freedom,
breaking from addiction

An overabundance of materialism

his bounds to luxury
must keep him restrained.
living in constant fear.

he keeps his dominion.
over your discretion,
do not let him cage you.

THE STARS

What do you imagine,
When you're on your own,
needing a distraction,
seeking the unknown?

I'll tell you what I see,
keep it just with you,
Dreams in obscurity,
Of us draped in blue.

In the starry night sky,
Two of us soaring,
In love and so high,
We were exploring.

So close yet so far away,
immersed in fantasy,
just friends where we lay,
Pain like ecstasy.

Silvery stars sparkle,
not as bright as you,
feelings had me startled,

lashes wet with dew.
When you hold my hand,
God, I feel alive,
you will not understand,
the love that will thrive.

Just a fool to pretend,
She sees me as I am,
or more than a girl friend
just a sorry sham.

Can you breathe up there without me?
like those suffocating stars.
I'll be your willing abductee,
Staying behind these cold bars

I'll tell you what I see,
Games I hate to play,
Dreams in obscurity,
See us cold in grey.

In the pitch-black sky,
Two of us roaring,
In pain and so high,
I'm discolouring.

THE FORBIDDEN

There is no reason to fear being free,
We fear letting go of ones we once
loved,
But that ache deep in the chest,
Our soul deeply shoved.

It hurts to know that laughter,
Towards the end was merely a ruse,
Fractured memories of comfort,
Left with an untreatable bruise.

It hurts to let them go,
Broken scissors sawing through rope,
But your happiness is dwindling,
You are struggling to cope.

You are more than a shell,
More than how you feel,
You are the strongest of the strong,
That love you have is always real.

Spend that love on someone,
Who will mend it back together,

No matter how broken it becomes,
It will always heal better.

THE BEACON

Rolling hills decked in white.
Smoke and fire fill the senses.
Wind icy and strong enough to bite.
The entire village looking apprehensive.

Trees frail from the cold.
Shadow's dancing, men trudged home.
Dogs trailing behind them sniffing at
mold.
Being intrigued by everything but never
far they roam

High in the sky crows swoop
Children giggling on the ground.
They laugh and twist turning in loops.
The thick ice perfect for spinning wildly
around.

Their kills lack quantity.
But it keeps families alive.
The hunters head towards the city
They are tired and weary but in the heat
of the hunt they thrive.

Everything is covered in frost,
An icy blue tint covers fingertips,
There is a fear that one will get lost,
The worry stirs when only one man
loses footing and slips.

EQUILIBRIUM

Life is all about balance,
Who and what you will keep,
Happiness will ebb and flow,
Try new tricks, steady it.

There will be many people,
Who come into your life,
Some will provide clarity,
Others are a hindrance.

Are you a charmer?
Perhaps a jester?
Or even divine,
Your goal to be kind.

To be yourself is something wonderful,
Do not let others impede on your peace,
Your search for balance is yours,
Do not fear your freedom.

You will find fruition.
You will see the bright stars.
You will hold your soulmate.

You will live in comfort.

Peace,
And Love,
Will always,
Follow.

www.ingramcontent.com/pod-product-compliance
Lightning Source LLC
La Vergne TN
LVHW021719210726
843509LV00021B/2595